50 Savory and Sweet Crepes

By: Kelly Johnson

Table of Contents

- Classic French Crepes
- Nutella and Banana Crepes
- Ham and Cheese Crepes
- Spinach and Ricotta Crepes
- Mushroom and Swiss Cheese Crepes
- Lemon and Sugar Crepes
- Apple Cinnamon Crepes
- Chicken Alfredo Crepes
- Smoked Salmon and Cream Cheese Crepes
- Strawberry and Cream Crepes
- Bacon and Egg Crepes
- Blueberry and Mascarpone Crepes
- Tomato Basil Crepes
- Chocolate Hazelnut Crepes
- Shrimp and Avocado Crepes
- Caramelized Banana Crepes
- Beef Stroganoff Crepes
- Pear and Gorgonzola Crepes
- Peaches and Cream Crepes
- Spinach and Feta Crepes
- Pecan Pie Crepes
- Mediterranean Veggie Crepes
- Sweet Potato and Goat Cheese Crepes
- Pineapple and Coconut Crepes
- Pulled Pork and Coleslaw Crepes
- Churro Crepes
- Roasted Veggie Crepes
- Cream Cheese and Jelly Crepes
- Chicken Caesar Crepes
- Meringue and Berry Crepes
- BBQ Chicken Crepes
- Pistachio and Honey Crepes
- Prosciutto and Melon Crepes
- Raspberry and Almond Crepes
- Smoked Salmon and Cucumber Crepes

- Tiramisu Crepes
- Mediterranean Chicken Crepes
- Nutty Chocolate Crepes
- Sausage and Peppers Crepes
- Apple Pie Crepes
- Lobster and Garlic Butter Crepes
- S'mores Crepes
- Fig and Ricotta Crepes
- Broccoli and Cheddar Crepes
- Apricot Jam and Cream Crepes
- Prawn and Garlic Butter Crepes
- Blackberry and Honey Crepes
- Sweet Cream and Strawberries Crepes
- Zucchini and Mozzarella Crepes
- Cinnamon Roll Crepes

Classic French Crepes

Ingredients:

- 1 cup all-purpose flour
- 2 eggs
- ½ cup milk
- ½ cup water
- ¼ teaspoon salt
- 2 tablespoons melted butter

Instructions:

1. In a mixing bowl, whisk together the flour and eggs.
2. Gradually add the milk and water, stirring to combine.
3. Add the salt and melted butter, whisking until smooth.
4. Heat a lightly oiled non-stick pan over medium-high heat.
5. Pour ¼ cup of batter into the pan, swirling to coat the surface evenly.
6. Cook for about 2 minutes, then flip and cook for another minute.
7. Remove from the pan and repeat with the remaining batter.
8. Serve warm with sweet or savory fillings.

Nutella and Banana Crepes

Ingredients:

- 1 cup all-purpose flour
- 2 eggs
- 1 cup milk
- ½ cup water
- 2 tbsp melted butter
- 1 tbsp sugar
- 1 tsp vanilla extract
- ¼ tsp salt
- ½ cup Nutella
- 2 bananas, sliced
- Powdered sugar (for dusting)

Instructions:

1. In a mixing bowl, whisk together the flour, eggs, milk, water, melted butter, sugar, vanilla, and salt until smooth.
2. Heat a non-stick skillet over medium heat and lightly grease with butter.
3. Pour about ¼ cup of batter into the skillet, swirling to coat the bottom evenly.
4. Cook for about 1-2 minutes until the edges lift slightly, then flip and cook for another 30 seconds.
5. Remove the crepe, spread Nutella over one half, and layer with banana slices.
6. Fold the crepe in half, then again into a triangle.
7. Dust with powdered sugar and serve warm.

Ham and Cheese Crepes

Ingredients:

- 1 cup all-purpose flour
- 2 eggs
- 1 cup milk
- ½ cup water
- 2 tbsp melted butter
- ¼ tsp salt
- ½ cup shredded Gruyère or Swiss cheese
- 4 slices ham
- 1 tbsp Dijon mustard (optional)
- Fresh parsley (for garnish)

Instructions:

1. In a bowl, whisk together the flour, eggs, milk, water, melted butter, and salt until smooth.
2. Heat a non-stick skillet over medium heat and lightly grease with butter.
3. Pour ¼ cup of batter into the skillet, swirling to spread evenly.
4. Cook for 1-2 minutes until the edges lift, then flip and cook for another 30 seconds.
5. Place a slice of ham and a sprinkle of cheese on one half of the crepe.
6. Fold the crepe over the filling and cook for 30 seconds until the cheese melts.
7. Remove from heat, drizzle with Dijon mustard if desired, and garnish with parsley.

Spinach and Ricotta Crepes

Ingredients:

- 1 cup all-purpose flour
- 2 eggs
- 1 cup milk
- ½ cup water
- 2 tbsp melted butter
- ¼ tsp salt
- 1 cup fresh spinach, chopped
- ½ cup ricotta cheese
- ¼ cup grated Parmesan
- 1 garlic clove, minced
- ¼ tsp ground nutmeg
- Salt and pepper to taste

Instructions:

1. In a bowl, mix the flour, eggs, milk, water, melted butter, and salt until smooth.
2. Heat a non-stick skillet over medium heat and lightly grease with butter.
3. Pour ¼ cup of batter into the skillet, swirling to coat the bottom.
4. Cook for about 1-2 minutes, flip, and cook for another 30 seconds.
5. In a separate pan, sauté garlic and spinach until wilted.
6. In a bowl, mix the cooked spinach with ricotta, Parmesan, nutmeg, salt, and pepper.
7. Spoon the filling onto one side of the crepe, fold over, and serve warm.

Mushroom and Swiss Cheese Crepes

Ingredients:

- 1 cup all-purpose flour
- 2 eggs
- 1 cup milk
- ½ cup water
- 2 tbsp melted butter
- ¼ tsp salt
- 1 tbsp olive oil
- 1 cup mushrooms, sliced
- 1 garlic clove, minced
- ½ cup shredded Swiss cheese
- Salt and pepper to taste
- Fresh thyme (for garnish)

Instructions:

1. Prepare the crepe batter by whisking flour, eggs, milk, water, melted butter, and salt until smooth.
2. Heat a skillet over medium heat, add olive oil, and sauté mushrooms with garlic until tender. Season with salt and pepper.
3. Cook the crepes by pouring ¼ cup batter into a greased skillet, swirling to spread evenly. Cook for 1-2 minutes per side.
4. Fill each crepe with sautéed mushrooms and Swiss cheese, then fold.
5. Garnish with fresh thyme and serve warm.

Lemon and Sugar Crepes

Ingredients:

- 1 cup all-purpose flour
- 2 eggs
- 1 cup milk
- ½ cup water
- 2 tbsp melted butter
- ¼ tsp salt
- 2 tbsp granulated sugar
- 1 lemon, zested and juiced
- Powdered sugar (for dusting)

Instructions:

1. Whisk together the flour, eggs, milk, water, melted butter, and salt until smooth.
2. Cook thin crepes in a greased skillet over medium heat, flipping after 1-2 minutes.
3. Sprinkle each crepe with granulated sugar and drizzle with fresh lemon juice.
4. Fold and dust with powdered sugar before serving.

Apple Cinnamon Crepes

Ingredients:

- 1 cup all-purpose flour
- 2 eggs
- 1 cup milk
- ½ cup water
- 2 tbsp melted butter
- ¼ tsp salt
- 2 apples, peeled and diced
- 2 tbsp butter
- 2 tbsp brown sugar
- 1 tsp cinnamon
- ¼ tsp nutmeg

Instructions:

1. In a pan, melt butter and sauté apples with brown sugar, cinnamon, and nutmeg until soft.
2. Prepare crepes using standard batter and cook until golden.
3. Fill crepes with warm apple mixture, fold, and serve.

Chicken Alfredo Crepes

Ingredients:

- 1 cup all-purpose flour
- 2 eggs
- 1 cup milk
- ½ cup water
- 2 tbsp melted butter
- ¼ tsp salt
- 1 cup cooked shredded chicken
- ½ cup Alfredo sauce
- ½ cup shredded mozzarella
- 1 tbsp fresh parsley (for garnish)

Instructions:

1. Cook crepes in a greased skillet over medium heat.
2. Warm the chicken with Alfredo sauce and mozzarella.
3. Fill crepes with the chicken mixture, fold, and top with fresh parsley.

Smoked Salmon and Cream Cheese Crepes

Ingredients:

- 1 cup all-purpose flour
- 2 eggs
- 1 cup milk
- ½ cup water
- 2 tbsp melted butter
- ¼ tsp salt
- ½ cup cream cheese, softened
- 4 oz smoked salmon
- 1 tbsp fresh dill
- 1 tsp capers (optional)

Instructions:

1. Prepare and cook crepes until golden brown.
2. Spread each crepe with cream cheese, top with smoked salmon, dill, and capers.
3. Fold and serve immediately.

Strawberry and Cream Crepes

Ingredients:

- 1 cup all-purpose flour
- 2 eggs
- 1 cup milk
- ½ cup water
- 2 tbsp melted butter
- ¼ tsp salt
- 1 cup strawberries, sliced
- ½ cup whipped cream
- 2 tbsp powdered sugar

Instructions:

1. Prepare and cook crepes until golden.
2. Fill with fresh strawberries and whipped cream.
3. Fold, dust with powdered sugar, and serve.

Bacon and Egg Crepes

Ingredients:

- 1 cup all-purpose flour
- 2 eggs
- 1 cup milk
- ½ cup water
- 2 tbsp melted butter
- ¼ tsp salt
- 4 slices bacon, cooked and crumbled
- 2 eggs, scrambled
- ½ cup shredded cheddar cheese

Instructions:

1. Prepare and cook crepes.
2. Fill with scrambled eggs, bacon, and cheese.
3. Fold and serve warm.

Blueberry and Mascarpone Crepes

Ingredients:

- 1 cup all-purpose flour
- 2 eggs
- 1 cup milk
- ½ cup water
- 2 tbsp melted butter
- ¼ tsp salt
- ½ cup mascarpone cheese
- 1 cup fresh blueberries
- 2 tbsp honey

Instructions:

1. Cook crepes and set aside.
2. Spread mascarpone cheese inside each crepe, add blueberries, and drizzle with honey.
3. Fold and serve.

Tomato Basil Crepes

Ingredients:

- 1 cup all-purpose flour
- 2 eggs
- 1 cup milk
- ½ cup water
- 2 tbsp melted butter
- ¼ tsp salt
- ½ cup cherry tomatoes, halved
- ¼ cup fresh basil, chopped
- ½ cup mozzarella cheese

Instructions:

1. Prepare and cook crepes.
2. Fill with cherry tomatoes, fresh basil, and mozzarella cheese.
3. Fold and serve warm.

Chocolate Hazelnut Crepes

Ingredients:

- 1 cup all-purpose flour
- 2 eggs
- 1 cup milk
- ½ cup water
- 2 tbsp melted butter
- ¼ tsp salt
- ½ cup chocolate hazelnut spread
- ¼ cup chopped hazelnuts
- Powdered sugar (for garnish)

Instructions:

1. Cook crepes and let them cool slightly.
2. Spread chocolate hazelnut spread inside each crepe.
3. Sprinkle with chopped hazelnuts, fold, and dust with powdered sugar before serving.

Shrimp and Avocado Crepes

Ingredients:

- 1 cup all-purpose flour
- 2 eggs
- 1 cup milk
- ½ cup water
- 2 tbsp melted butter
- ¼ tsp salt
- 1 cup cooked shrimp, chopped
- 1 avocado, sliced
- ½ cup sour cream
- 1 tbsp lime juice
- 1 tbsp fresh cilantro, chopped

Instructions:

1. Prepare and cook crepes until golden.
2. In a bowl, mix sour cream with lime juice.
3. Fill crepes with shrimp and avocado, drizzle with lime sour cream, and sprinkle with cilantro.
4. Fold and serve.

Caramelized Banana Crepes

Ingredients:

- 1 cup all-purpose flour
- 2 eggs
- 1 cup milk
- ½ cup water
- 2 tbsp melted butter
- ¼ tsp salt
- 2 bananas, sliced
- 2 tbsp butter
- ¼ cup brown sugar
- ½ tsp cinnamon

Instructions:

1. Prepare and cook crepes.
2. In a pan, melt butter and cook bananas with brown sugar and cinnamon until caramelized.
3. Fill crepes with caramelized bananas, fold, and serve.

Beef Stroganoff Crepes

Ingredients:

- 1 cup all-purpose flour
- 2 eggs
- 1 cup milk
- ½ cup water
- 2 tbsp melted butter
- ¼ tsp salt
- 1 cup cooked beef strips
- ½ cup mushrooms, sliced
- ½ cup sour cream
- 1 tbsp Dijon mustard
- 1 tbsp fresh parsley

Instructions:

1. Cook crepes until golden and set aside.
2. Sauté mushrooms in a pan, add beef, then stir in sour cream and mustard.
3. Fill crepes with beef mixture, fold, and garnish with parsley.

Pear and Gorgonzola Crepes

Ingredients:

- 1 cup all-purpose flour
- 2 eggs
- 1 cup milk
- ½ cup water
- 2 tbsp melted butter
- ¼ tsp salt
- 1 pear, thinly sliced
- ½ cup crumbled Gorgonzola cheese
- 2 tbsp honey
- ¼ cup chopped walnuts

Instructions:

1. Prepare and cook crepes.
2. Fill each crepe with pear slices and Gorgonzola.
3. Drizzle with honey and top with walnuts before folding and serving.

Peaches and Cream Crepes

Ingredients:

- 1 cup all-purpose flour
- 2 eggs
- 1 cup milk
- ½ cup water
- 2 tbsp melted butter
- ¼ tsp salt
- 1 cup sliced peaches
- ½ cup whipped cream
- 1 tbsp honey

Instructions:

1. Cook crepes and let cool slightly.
2. Fill each crepe with peaches and whipped cream.
3. Drizzle with honey, fold, and serve.

Spinach and Feta Crepes

Ingredients:

- 1 cup all-purpose flour
- 2 eggs
- 1 cup milk
- ½ cup water
- 2 tbsp melted butter
- ¼ tsp salt
- 1 cup fresh spinach, chopped
- ½ cup crumbled feta cheese
- 1 garlic clove, minced

Instructions:

1. Sauté spinach and garlic until wilted.
2. Cook crepes until golden.
3. Fill with spinach and feta, fold, and serve.

Pecan Pie Crepes

Ingredients:

- 1 cup all-purpose flour
- 2 eggs
- 1 cup milk
- ½ cup water
- 2 tbsp melted butter
- ¼ tsp salt
- ½ cup chopped pecans
- ¼ cup brown sugar
- 2 tbsp butter
- ½ tsp cinnamon
- 2 tbsp maple syrup

Instructions:

1. Cook crepes until golden.
2. In a pan, melt butter and cook pecans with brown sugar and cinnamon.
3. Fill crepes with pecan mixture, drizzle with maple syrup, fold, and serve.

Mediterranean Veggie Crepes

Ingredients:

- 1 cup all-purpose flour
- 2 eggs
- 1 cup milk
- ½ cup water
- 2 tbsp melted butter
- ¼ tsp salt
- ½ cup roasted red peppers, chopped
- ½ cup zucchini, diced
- ¼ cup crumbled feta cheese
- 1 tbsp olive oil
- ½ tsp oregano

Instructions:

1. Sauté red peppers and zucchini in olive oil with oregano.
2. Cook crepes and fill with veggie mixture and feta.
3. Fold and serve.

Sweet Potato and Goat Cheese Crepes

Ingredients:

- 1 cup all-purpose flour
- 2 eggs
- 1 cup milk
- ½ cup water
- 2 tbsp melted butter
- ¼ tsp salt
- 1 cup mashed sweet potatoes
- ½ cup goat cheese
- 1 tbsp honey

Instructions:

1. Cook crepes and set aside.
2. Spread sweet potatoes inside each crepe, sprinkle with goat cheese, and drizzle with honey.
3. Fold and serve warm.

Pineapple and Coconut Crepes

Ingredients:

- 1 cup all-purpose flour
- 2 eggs
- 1 cup milk
- ½ cup water
- 2 tbsp melted butter
- ¼ tsp salt
- 1 cup diced pineapple
- ¼ cup shredded coconut
- 2 tbsp honey

Instructions:

1. Cook crepes and let cool slightly.
2. Fill with pineapple and coconut, drizzle with honey, and fold before serving.

Pulled Pork and Coleslaw Crepes

Ingredients:

- 1 cup all-purpose flour
- 2 eggs
- 1 cup milk
- ½ cup water
- 2 tbsp melted butter
- ¼ tsp salt
- 1 cup cooked pulled pork
- ½ cup barbecue sauce
- 1 cup coleslaw
- 1 tbsp chopped fresh cilantro

Instructions:

1. Cook crepes and set aside.
2. Warm pulled pork with barbecue sauce.
3. Fill crepes with pulled pork and coleslaw, fold, and garnish with cilantro.

Churro Crepes

Ingredients:

- 1 cup all-purpose flour
- 2 eggs
- 1 cup milk
- ½ cup water
- 2 tbsp melted butter
- ¼ tsp salt
- ¼ cup granulated sugar
- 1 tsp cinnamon
- ¼ cup melted butter (for brushing)

Instructions:

1. Cook crepes until golden.
2. Mix sugar and cinnamon in a bowl.
3. Brush each crepe with melted butter, sprinkle with cinnamon sugar, fold, and serve.

Roasted Veggie Crepes

Ingredients:

- 1 cup all-purpose flour
- 2 eggs
- 1 cup milk
- ½ cup water
- 2 tbsp melted butter
- ¼ tsp salt
- ½ cup zucchini, diced
- ½ cup bell peppers, sliced
- ½ cup cherry tomatoes, halved
- 1 tbsp olive oil
- ½ tsp dried thyme
- ½ cup crumbled goat cheese

Instructions:

1. Roast zucchini, bell peppers, and tomatoes with olive oil and thyme until tender.
2. Cook crepes and fill with roasted veggies and goat cheese.
3. Fold and serve warm.

Cream Cheese and Jelly Crepes

Ingredients:

- 1 cup all-purpose flour
- 2 eggs
- 1 cup milk
- ½ cup water
- 2 tbsp melted butter
- ¼ tsp salt
- ½ cup cream cheese
- ¼ cup favorite fruit jelly

Instructions:

1. Cook crepes and let cool slightly.
2. Spread cream cheese and jelly inside each crepe, fold, and serve.

Chicken Caesar Crepes

Ingredients:

- 1 cup all-purpose flour
- 2 eggs
- 1 cup milk
- ½ cup water
- 2 tbsp melted butter
- ¼ tsp salt
- 1 cup cooked shredded chicken
- ¼ cup Caesar dressing
- ½ cup chopped romaine lettuce
- ¼ cup grated Parmesan cheese

Instructions:

1. Mix chicken with Caesar dressing.
2. Cook crepes and fill with chicken, lettuce, and Parmesan.
3. Fold and serve.

Meringue and Berry Crepes

Ingredients:

- 1 cup all-purpose flour
- 2 eggs
- 1 cup milk
- ½ cup water
- 2 tbsp melted butter
- ¼ tsp salt
- 1 cup fresh mixed berries
- ½ cup meringue pieces
- 2 tbsp honey

Instructions:

1. Cook crepes and set aside.
2. Fill each crepe with fresh berries and crumbled meringue.
3. Drizzle with honey, fold, and serve.

BBQ Chicken Crepes

Ingredients:

- 1 cup all-purpose flour
- 2 eggs
- 1 cup milk
- ½ cup water
- 2 tbsp melted butter
- ¼ tsp salt
- 1 cup cooked shredded chicken
- ½ cup barbecue sauce
- ½ cup shredded cheddar cheese

Instructions:

1. Warm chicken with barbecue sauce.
2. Cook crepes and fill with BBQ chicken and cheese.
3. Fold and serve warm.

Pistachio and Honey Crepes

Ingredients:

- 1 cup all-purpose flour
- 2 eggs
- 1 cup milk
- ½ cup water
- 2 tbsp melted butter
- ¼ tsp salt
- ½ cup chopped pistachios
- 2 tbsp honey
- ½ cup whipped cream

Instructions:

1. Cook crepes and let cool slightly.
2. Fill with whipped cream and chopped pistachios.
3. Drizzle with honey, fold, and serve.

Prosciutto and Melon Crepes

Ingredients:

- 1 cup all-purpose flour
- 2 eggs
- 1 cup milk
- ½ cup water
- 2 tbsp melted butter
- ¼ tsp salt
- 4 slices prosciutto
- 1 cup cantaloupe, thinly sliced
- ½ cup arugula

Instructions:

1. Cook crepes and set aside.
2. Fill each crepe with prosciutto, melon slices, and arugula.
3. Fold and serve.

Raspberry and Almond Crepes

Ingredients:

- 1 cup all-purpose flour
- 2 eggs
- 1 cup milk
- ½ cup water
- 2 tbsp melted butter
- ¼ tsp salt
- 1 cup fresh raspberries
- ¼ cup sliced almonds
- 2 tbsp honey

Instructions:

1. Cook crepes and let cool slightly.
2. Fill with raspberries and sliced almonds.
3. Drizzle with honey, fold, and serve.

Smoked Salmon and Cucumber Crepes

Ingredients:

- 1 cup all-purpose flour
- 2 eggs
- 1 cup milk
- ½ cup water
- 2 tbsp melted butter
- ¼ tsp salt
- 4 oz smoked salmon
- ½ cup cucumber, thinly sliced
- ½ cup cream cheese
- 1 tbsp fresh dill

Instructions:

1. Cook crepes and set aside.
2. Spread cream cheese inside each crepe and layer with smoked salmon and cucumber.
3. Sprinkle with fresh dill, fold, and serve.

Tiramisu Crepes

Ingredients:

- 1 cup all-purpose flour
- 2 eggs
- 1 cup milk
- ½ cup water
- 2 tbsp melted butter
- ¼ tsp salt
- ½ cup mascarpone cheese
- 2 tbsp sugar
- ½ tsp vanilla extract
- 1 tbsp espresso, cooled
- 2 tbsp cocoa powder
- ½ cup whipped cream

Instructions:

1. Cook crepes and let cool.
2. Mix mascarpone, sugar, vanilla, and espresso until smooth.
3. Fill crepes with mascarpone mixture, fold, and dust with cocoa powder.
4. Top with whipped cream before serving.

Mediterranean Chicken Crepes

Ingredients:

- 1 cup all-purpose flour
- 2 eggs
- 1 cup milk
- ½ cup water
- 2 tbsp melted butter
- ¼ tsp salt
- 1 cup cooked shredded chicken
- ½ cup diced tomatoes
- ¼ cup Kalamata olives, sliced
- ½ cup crumbled feta cheese
- 1 tbsp olive oil
- ½ tsp dried oregano

Instructions:

1. Sauté chicken, tomatoes, olives, and oregano in olive oil.
2. Cook crepes and fill with the mixture.
3. Sprinkle with feta cheese, fold, and serve.

Nutty Chocolate Crepes

Ingredients:

- 1 cup all-purpose flour
- 2 eggs
- 1 cup milk
- ½ cup water
- 2 tbsp melted butter
- ¼ tsp salt
- ½ cup chocolate hazelnut spread
- ¼ cup chopped almonds
- ¼ cup chopped hazelnuts
- Powdered sugar (for garnish)

Instructions:

1. Cook crepes and let cool slightly.
2. Spread chocolate hazelnut spread inside each crepe.
3. Sprinkle with almonds and hazelnuts, fold, and dust with powdered sugar.

Sausage and Peppers Crepes

Ingredients:

- 1 cup all-purpose flour
- 2 eggs
- 1 cup milk
- ½ cup water
- 2 tbsp melted butter
- ¼ tsp salt
- 1 cup cooked Italian sausage, sliced
- ½ cup bell peppers, sliced
- ½ cup onions, sliced
- 1 tbsp olive oil
- ½ cup shredded mozzarella

Instructions:

1. Sauté sausage, peppers, and onions in olive oil until tender.
2. Cook crepes and fill with the mixture.
3. Sprinkle with mozzarella, fold, and serve warm.

Apple Pie Crepes

Ingredients:

- 1 cup all-purpose flour
- 2 eggs
- 1 cup milk
- ½ cup water
- 2 tbsp melted butter
- ¼ tsp salt
- 2 apples, peeled and diced
- 2 tbsp butter
- 2 tbsp brown sugar
- 1 tsp cinnamon
- ¼ tsp nutmeg

Instructions:

1. Sauté apples with butter, brown sugar, cinnamon, and nutmeg until soft.
2. Cook crepes and fill with the apple mixture.
3. Fold and serve warm.

Lobster and Garlic Butter Crepes

Ingredients:

- 1 cup all-purpose flour
- 2 eggs
- 1 cup milk
- ½ cup water
- 2 tbsp melted butter
- ¼ tsp salt
- 1 cup cooked lobster meat, chopped
- 2 tbsp butter
- 1 garlic clove, minced
- ½ cup heavy cream
- ¼ tsp lemon zest
- 1 tbsp fresh parsley

Instructions:

1. Sauté garlic in butter, then add lobster and heavy cream.
2. Cook crepes and fill with the mixture.
3. Garnish with lemon zest and parsley before serving.

S'mores Crepes

Ingredients:

- 1 cup all-purpose flour
- 2 eggs
- 1 cup milk
- ½ cup water
- 2 tbsp melted butter
- ¼ tsp salt
- ½ cup chocolate chips
- ½ cup mini marshmallows
- ¼ cup crushed graham crackers

Instructions:

1. Cook crepes and let cool slightly.
2. Fill with chocolate chips and marshmallows, then fold.
3. Sprinkle with crushed graham crackers before serving.

Fig and Ricotta Crepes

Ingredients:

- 1 cup all-purpose flour
- 2 eggs
- 1 cup milk
- ½ cup water
- 2 tbsp melted butter
- ¼ tsp salt
- ½ cup ricotta cheese
- 4 fresh figs, sliced
- 2 tbsp honey
- ¼ cup chopped walnuts

Instructions:

1. Cook crepes and set aside.
2. Fill with ricotta and sliced figs.
3. Drizzle with honey and sprinkle with walnuts before serving.

Broccoli and Cheddar Crepes

Ingredients:

- 1 cup all-purpose flour
- 2 eggs
- 1 cup milk
- ½ cup water
- 2 tbsp melted butter
- ¼ tsp salt
- 1 cup broccoli florets, chopped
- ½ cup shredded cheddar cheese
- 1 tbsp butter
- 1 garlic clove, minced
- ¼ cup heavy cream

Instructions:

1. Sauté broccoli and garlic in butter until tender.
2. Stir in heavy cream and cheddar cheese until melted.
3. Cook crepes and fill with broccoli mixture.
4. Fold and serve warm.

Apricot Jam and Cream Crepes

Ingredients:

- 1 cup all-purpose flour
- 2 eggs
- 1 cup milk
- ½ cup water
- 2 tbsp melted butter
- ¼ tsp salt
- ½ cup apricot jam
- ½ cup whipped cream

Instructions:

1. Cook crepes and let cool slightly.
2. Spread apricot jam inside each crepe.
3. Add a dollop of whipped cream, fold, and serve.

Prawn and Garlic Butter Crepes

Ingredients:

- 1 cup all-purpose flour
- 2 eggs
- 1 cup milk
- ½ cup water
- 2 tbsp melted butter
- ¼ tsp salt
- 1 cup cooked prawns, chopped
- 2 tbsp butter
- 1 garlic clove, minced
- ½ cup heavy cream
- 1 tbsp fresh parsley

Instructions:

1. Sauté garlic in butter, then add prawns and heavy cream.
2. Cook crepes and fill with prawn mixture.
3. Garnish with parsley before serving.

Blackberry and Honey Crepes

Ingredients:

- 1 cup all-purpose flour
- 2 eggs
- 1 cup milk
- ½ cup water
- 2 tbsp melted butter
- ¼ tsp salt
- 1 cup fresh blackberries
- 2 tbsp honey
- ½ cup whipped cream

Instructions:

1. Cook crepes and let cool slightly.
2. Fill with blackberries and drizzle with honey.
3. Add whipped cream, fold, and serve.

Sweet Cream and Strawberries Crepes

Ingredients:

- 1 cup all-purpose flour
- 2 eggs
- 1 cup milk
- ½ cup water
- 2 tbsp melted butter
- ¼ tsp salt
- 1 cup sliced strawberries
- ½ cup heavy cream
- 2 tbsp sugar

Instructions:

1. Whip heavy cream with sugar until soft peaks form.
2. Cook crepes and let cool slightly.
3. Fill with sweet cream and strawberries, fold, and serve.

Zucchini and Mozzarella Crepes

Ingredients:

- 1 cup all-purpose flour
- 2 eggs
- 1 cup milk
- ½ cup water
- 2 tbsp melted butter
- ¼ tsp salt
- 1 cup zucchini, shredded
- ½ cup shredded mozzarella
- 1 tbsp olive oil
- ½ tsp dried oregano

Instructions:

1. Sauté zucchini in olive oil with oregano until soft.
2. Cook crepes and fill with zucchini and mozzarella.
3. Fold and serve warm.

Cinnamon Roll Crepes

Ingredients:

- 1 cup all-purpose flour
- 2 eggs
- 1 cup milk
- ½ cup water
- 2 tbsp melted butter
- ¼ tsp salt
- ¼ cup brown sugar
- 1 tsp cinnamon
- 2 tbsp melted butter (for filling)
- ½ cup cream cheese frosting

Instructions:

1. Cook crepes and let cool slightly.
2. Mix brown sugar and cinnamon with melted butter, then spread inside each crepe.
3. Drizzle with cream cheese frosting, fold, and serve.

www.ingramcontent.com/pod-product-compliance
Lightning Source LLC
LaVergne TN
LVHW081503060526
838201LV00056BA/2900